TABLE OF CONTENTS

Phase One: Pathway to Destruction

Day 1 — Will You Accept This Challenge

Day 2 — Her Heartbeat

Day 3 — Pure

Day 4 — Forever and Always (Part 1)

Day 5 — Forever & Always (Part 2)

Day 6 — Modern Day King

Day 7 — 42 Seconds

Day 8 — Royal Strangers

Day 9 — Black Is …

Day 10 — Rumble King Rumble

Phase Two: Destruction & Anger

Day 11 — What Do You See?

Day 12 — Art of War

Day 13 — Namaste

Day 14 — Feel Me Deep

Day 15 — Soul

Day 16 — Hands Up Don't Shoot

Day 17 — Roots

Day 18 — Reflection

Day 19 — Manifestation

Day 20 — Freedom

Phase Three: Growth & Healing

Day 21 — Sand

Day 22 — Waves

Day 23 — Process and Pain

Day 24 — Wake Up America

Day 25 — Lion's Roar

Day 26 — I Am King

Day 27 — Cheers

Day 28 — Legacy

Day 29 — Victory

Day 30 — Reflection (Part 2)

Day 31 — Black Man

Day 32 — Scars

Day 33 — Sacrifice

Day 34 — Three Years Ago

Day 35 — Mastermind

Day 36 — Let It Burn

Day 37 — Flawed Not

Day 38 — The Wrong Right One

Day 39 — Let It Go

Day 40 — Peace, Love, Joy, and Life

Day 41 — True Love

Day 42 — Dear America ...

Final Reflections & Gratitude

DEDICATION

"To those on the jaded path of healing, you are loved, seen, and heard.

May you find peace through the tears."

— Duane E. Davis II

INTRODUCTION

This book is a collection of writings and inner thoughts I've created over the years.

They have been carefully curated to portray the true essence and nature of my heart.

It is a journey of the inner monolog I have had while in those dark days and quiet moments of reflection.

It is a collection of experiences in my life, and of life through the eyes of a person with a dream to create.

It is passion, it is love, it is pain, it is growth, and it is peace.

It is my journey through love.

It is authentically me.

— Duane

HOW TO USE THIS JOURNAL

This devotional journal is designed to help you move through your healing journey one day at a time. Each daily entry includes:

1. **The Original Poem**

Every poem is presented exactly as written — raw, honest, and unaltered.

These are gateways into reflection, emotional awareness, and spiritual grounding.

2. **Reflection & Application**

Guided prompts to help you explore what the poem brings up within you:

insight, memory, challenge, or growth.

3. **Daily Affirmation**

A short, empowering statement to re-center your energy and intention.

4. **Meditation Thought**

A universal spiritual reminder designed to help you breathe, reconnect, and reset.

5. **Journaling Space**

Use this space to write freely.

Allow your thoughts to flow without judgment.

Your healing lives in your expression.

Move at your own pace. You may take one entry per day or sit with a single day for a week.

There is no rush — only presence. This is your journey.

Your healing. Your transformation.

PHASE ONE

PATHWAY TO DESTRUCTION

DAY 1 — WILL YOU ACCEPT THIS CHALLENGE

Poem:

Our streets are crying out paved with blood of lost souls

Red, white, and blue once stood for unity, now we fight those colors against each other for our chance at meaningless gold

Our culture is becoming extinct, but we cannot only blame the lighter skin

Your dealer was black, your killer was black, this time the lighter skin is on the outside laughing while looking in

When my mother was a child, and her mother was a child, they were not ashamed to hide their hate

As time passed on, they learned to put knowledge in books, give us distractions, and puppet master our fate

Self-inflicted genocide when we choose guns over books

Someone please tell me, how many more funerals must we attend before we stop biting the same hook

The system won't change, the cycle continues from generation to generation

All it takes is one to know they possess the power to wake a sleeping nation

Stand firm with your chest out because the lion of Judah gives you strength to handle

Go back to that hood and wake the others is your mission ignite the candle

This challenge is simple, love your community, a task I know we can manage

But first I must know, will you accept this challenge?

Reflection & Application:

What role do you feel called to play in healing your community or your circle of influence?

Where is life challenging you to speak up, take action, or grow?

Daily Affirmation:

I stand in purpose, courage, and clarity.

Meditation Thought:

When I rise, my community rises with me.

_____

_____

_____

_____

_____

DAY 2 — HER HEARTBEAT

Poem:

Her heartbeat is the muse that inspires my ink to flow

Her touch is the river waters of love in my veins that waters my soul

Her words are the soil in which my roots form, and together we grow a legacy that withstands time and nature

My blessing is my burden and my burden is my gift

My vision of equality is past, present, and future facing tension it was built to resist

This gift that I've been given allows me to see inside of you what you don't yet see within yourself

So, the burden of my heart wants to join us as one, but your healing brings pain and drains me of my gift

Reflection & Application:

How do you honor your gift without losing your balance?

Where do you give too much of yourself? Where can you reclaim your energy?

Daily Affirmation:

My love has depth, but my peace has boundaries.

Meditation Thought:

Healing must flow both ways.

_____

_____

_____

_____

_____

DAY 3 — PURE

Poem:

I wish you could see what I see. Visions of a beautiful story being written through the purest form of art

I wish you could see what I see. A calming peace that overflows the deepest valleys of darkness

The drums of love that I hear echoing through the chambers of your heart become the soundtrack to our story of life

A story that fights to remain .... Pure

Reflection & Application:

Where in your life are you seeking purity — in intention, relationship, or purpose?

What does "remaining pure" mean to you spiritually or emotionally?

Daily Affirmation:

My heart remains clear, grounded, and aligned.

Meditation Thought:

Purity is the quiet truth beneath all chaos.

_____

_____

_____

_____

_____

DAY 4 — FOREVER AND ALWAYS (PART 1)

Poem:

A boldly nose with tears falling down her swollen face

His punches hurt but it was his words that brought her true disgrace

Last time she fell for his lies, thought the pain was pain

Now she finds herself in bloody tears, staring at the barrel of his shotgun

He said, "I love you, but I'll kill you if you think you're leaving me!

We said till death do us part and baby I meant that, seriously!"

She's thinking to herself, crying God how did I arrive here

On the highway to destruction stuck in high gear

From their first date to her wedding dress to the exotic honeymoon

She was proud to be his bride, and he was honored to be her groom

Somewhere down the line the darkness started to creep in

Shadows started choking out life, the demons made it hard for their love to breathe in

Candle lit dinners and his romance are now long gone

Replaced by black roses in a vase, rest in peace to their love now gone

Reflection & Application:

What cycles or patterns in your life have shifted from light to darkness?

Where do you need to reclaim your power or step away from what harms you?

Daily Affirmation:

I release what destroys my peace.

Meditation Thought:

Love is never meant to be painful, controlling, or deadly.

_____

_____

_____

_____

_____

DAY 5 — FOREVER & ALWAYS (PART 2)

Poem:

She starts to wonder to herself, am I worthy, does he truly love me

When I'm away at work, is he thinking of me

Am I beautiful even though I gained a little weight

Is he happy with the food I try to put on his plate

What is truly the issue, she's shedding tears trying to figure out

How he used to love her but now his heart has walked out

She wants your love and attention young king time to wake up

You're losing that good woman focused on rising your salary up

That man in her office, yep, he has his eyes on her

Snakes on a plane slither, he's getting close to comfort

Date one becomes date two, now he's stolen her heart

Careful now, she's falling for him, thinks this could be her brand new start

She's running home to pack her bags, he's the elevation she desires, no longer can she remain there

Her love is too valuable, her old life tossed away, love fades in the air

Now he refuses to let her go, which brings us back to the present

All I can do is pray that they both see the light, guide them before they wreck

Reflection & Application:

Where have doubts, insecurities, or unspoken needs created tension in your relationships?

What truth needs to be acknowledged within you today?

Daily Affirmation:

I honor my worth and protect my heart.

Meditation Thought:

Love cannot grow where truth is avoided.

_____

_____

_____

_____

_____

_____

DAY 6 — MODERN DAY KING

Poem:

He is the guy that is overlooked for being kind

He is the kind of guy that's really hard to find

He is the guy that's quietly on his grind, investing into others to make sure they get their shine

He is the man that's wise enough to be private but strong enough to be open

Against all odds he presses forward within his dreams, continuing to hope even when the world thinks of him as a joke

He is not perfect, but perfectly human

A man with flaws but steadily improving

Deliberate with his love so that there is no confusion

A one woman man, so any extra attention he constantly refuses

He raises his children even if they are not biologically his

He is his daughters first love

He teaches his son true humility which is a quality he learned from God that dwells within

He is an endangered species and a part of a dying breed

He does not allow life to slow him down, so with his chosen family by his side, he humbly leads

Some call him a decent man, some call him friend, some call him husband, some call him brother

Some call him mentor, some call him a leader

I choose to call him …. A modern day KING!

Reflection & Application:

Who are the "modern day kings" or quiet pillars in your life?

In what ways do you embody true royalty — not in title, but in character, service, and love?

Daily Affirmation:

My character, not my status, defines my crown.

Meditation Thought:

Royalty is revealed in how we love, serve, and lead.

_____

_____

_____

_____

_____

DAY 7 — 42 SECONDS

Poem:

42 seconds tick tock let the clock wind down

Right now, goal is to win your heart right now

No doubt, I see your pain when I look into your eyes

I want to help heal your heart, but this flesh is mesmerized by the sweet nectar between your thighs

Getting lost in the depth of your eyes butterflies carry me to destinations unknown

For I dwell in your spirit, your energy lifts me high, truth be told

Lustful nature of this flesh has me weak inside

I vow to be your knight in shining armor but secretly dying inside

Can you see the fire that burns, flames growing out of hand

Longing to live a peaceful life of calm rivers but the flesh reminds me I'm still a man

For I know the pain and the path to destiny is jaded

Broken heart pieces memories of joyful bliss have slowly faded

Never thought that this day would ever truly come

Kissing our final goodbyes realizing our love is done

Heart for the people but sometimes love can be my burden

Lies and hurt from those closest to me, I guess that's the burden of a servant

Reflection & Application:

Where do you feel pulled between desire and peace, between what you want and what you know is healthy?

What goodbyes or endings are still shaping your heart today?

Daily Affirmation:

I honor my humanity while choosing what nurtures my peace.

Meditation Thought:

Even when love ends, my purpose and capacity to love remains.

_____

_____

_____

_____

_____

DAY 8 — ROYAL STRANGERS

Poem:

Listen as my words open your eyes and realize that your perception to the world looks bad

In your feelings reminiscing on the good thing that you once thought you had

Came calling and crying because you thought I was still there

Our flame of love has faded to black now you get to watch me disappear

I wish we could go back to when we were strangers, but it's too late

Now you've seen my soul and built a place in my heart

Now you will forever be a part of me

As life moves on in our different directions, the spark and flame we once had slowly fades into a quiet stiff darkness, never to be lit again

If only we could be strangers once again

Back when we both lived life unaware of what the next few years would bring

Before the passions we once held suffered in silence as we drifted further apart

But it's too late now

If only we could be strangers once again

Reflection & Application:

What relationship in your life shifted from deep connection to distance?

What have you learned about yourself from loving someone you can no longer walk with?

Daily Affirmation:

I honor the love that was, and I release what no longer is.

Meditation Thought:

Not every soul that enters my life is meant to stay, but every connection can teach me something true.

_____

_____

_____

_____

_____

_____

DAY 9 — BLACK IS ...

Poem:

Black is bold. Black is beautiful. Black is peace. Black is joy. Black is out and feeling dangerous.

I am a force of destruction seeking to dismantle stereotypes, all walls built to limit me, and any perceived notions of who you may think I am.

Black is love. Black is power. Black is pain. Black is struggle. Black is war. Black is eternal. Black is strength. Black is wealth.

My mental fortitude, my knowledge of self, my peace, and my love makes me dangerous.

Reflection & Application:

What identities, roots, or stories make you who you are?

Where do you feel called to destroy false narratives about yourself or your people, and step fully into your truth?

Daily Affirmation:

I am powerful, intentional, and unashamed of who I am.

Meditation Thought:

Knowing myself is an act of liberation.

_____

_____

_____

_____

_____

_____

DAY 10 — RUMBLE KING RUMBLE

Poem:

Rumble Young King Rumble!

You're built to survive this concrete jungle! Speak when needed with your voice powerful as thunder! The essence of strength flowing through your veins pounds like the drums of your ancestors!

Peace becomes you like meditation by the still waters of the river Jordan! Agape Love dwells within your soul! You are built upon a legacy of royalty! Walk in light, dwell in peace, live in joy! You possess the spirit of ancient warriors who fight for truth, healing, and righteousness even if it means sacrificing their own lives!

You are KING!

Black man! Rumble Young King Rumble!

You were never meant to be a savage or a thug. That mentality was taught to you by white men who despise your masculinity.

You are a God by Nature!

You are strong and moral by Nature. You are kind, respectable, and merciful.

You are a product of peace and righteousness. Do not take on the identity of a beast to just deny your identity as a God.

Your royalty is in your righteousness!

Rumble Young King Rumble!

Reflection & Application:

Where have you shrunk yourself, forgotten your power, or accepted labels that never belonged to you?

What would it look like today to "rumble" — to rise, to walk in your true identity, and to live as royalty in how you think, move, and love?

Daily Affirmation:

I am royalty — my spirit, values, and choices reveal my crown.

Meditation Thought:

I don't have to become what the world fears; I can remain who I truly am.

_____

_____

_____

_____

_____

_____

PHASE TWO

DESTRUCTION & ANGER

DAY 11 — WHAT DO YOU SEE?

Poem:

Tell me, what do you see when you look at me?

The depth, essence, and passion of my soul is my legacy.

Do you see the struggles of the man, the fears and passions of the child, the insecurities of the flesh?

Do you see the determination to sacrifice it all for what is held close to heart until I exhale my last breath?

Tell me, what do you see when you look at me?

Do you see the pain, the scars, and the healing wounds that serve as motivation to push forward in my destiny?

Do you see the broken heart fighting for love on a jagged path refusing to let the world take what is left of me?

Do you see the aura of peace wrapped around my soul tight as a mother's love for her seed?

Do you see the joy I possess and the power of the ancestors I embrace with each moment I breathe?

Tell me, what do you see when you look at me?

Can you see the music pumping through my veins like a caged lion longing to be free?

Can you see the lifeline of art that saved my life when I was fighting for my sanity?

Do you see the heart to give, the heart to love, and the heart of the servant man?

My life is my legacy, and a King is who truly I am.

Tell me, what do you see when you look at me?

Reflection & Application:

How do you believe others see you — and how do you truly see yourself?

What parts of your story deserve more compassion, honor, or recognition?

Daily Affirmation:

I see myself clearly, fully, and truthfully.

Meditation Thought:

My story has depth, meaning, and purpose beyond first impressions.

_____

_____

_____

_____

_____

DAY 12 — ART OF WAR

Poem:

If you want peace, prepare for war

Silence in streets, proof of battle scars

We are forever living to thrive, for it is time to reap those seeds

Pain taught me to succeed, but first I had to bleed

Reflection & Application:

What internal or external battles have shaped your strength?

Where are you being called to protect your peace — even if it requires courage and confrontation?

Daily Affirmation:

My strength was forged through struggle, not by accident.

Meditation Thought:

Every scar carries wisdom.

_____

_____

_____

_____

_____

_____

DAY 13 — NAMASTE

Poem:

Speak for the voiceless

Fight for the fallen

Live for the ancestors

Breathe for those whose breath was taken too soon

The mission must continue

Reflection & Application:

Who or what do you feel called to stand for today?

How can your life honor those who came before you and those who can no longer speak?

Daily Affirmation:

My life is guided by purpose greater than myself.

Meditation Thought:

When I move with intention, I carry many souls with me.

_____

_____

_____

_____

_____

_____

DAY 14 — FEEL ME DEEP

Poem:

I will be the King you need. I'll conquer the land. To your seeds, I will be the example of a true man.

I will be the protector of your heart. I will be the love that feeds your soul.

I will be the pulse pumping through your veins that tells your heart that all men are not the same.

I will be the breath in your lungs. Inhale what's pure as I breathe life into you.

Your goals are mine, your dreams we share.

I will lay your body down and make love to you till our chakras intertwine into one dominant force of passion.

Feel me deep inside of you without physical penetration.

I'm a King serving his Queen, as we build our empire under the wisdom and guidance of THE KING.

Open your third eye and allow me to dwell.

Feel me deep inside of you without physical penetration.

That's the love I want. That's the love you deserve.

When we join as one, the ancestors rejoice with a thunderous roar.

The power of black souls beats louder than any ceremonial drum.

Feel me deep inside of you without physical penetration.

Reflection & Application:

What does deep connection mean to you beyond physical intimacy?

Where do you desire spiritual, emotional, or energetic unity in your life?

Daily Affirmation:

I am worthy of deep, conscious, and intentional love.

Meditation Thought:

True intimacy begins in the soul.

_____

_____

_____

_____

_____

DAY 15 — SOUL

Poem:

I need to taste the thoughts of your mind

I need to feel your thought process

Together we can unravel the intricate and intimate riddles of life

As our souls intertwine, caressing and memorizing each detail of perfection that makes us unique,

we shall soar through the cosmic dimensions of love,

defying the element of time with each stroke going deeper into the depths of our soul.

Reflection & Application:

Who do you feel most mentally and spiritually connected to?

How can you cultivate deeper understanding — with others and with yourself?

Daily Affirmation:

I value connection that reaches beyond the surface.

Meditation Thought:

When souls meet in truth, time becomes irrelevant.

_____

_____

_____

_____

_____

DAY 16 — HANDS UP DON'T SHOOT

Poem:

I hear those sirens in the nighttime

The wolves are out to prey

I hear those sirens in the nighttime

Ice blood flows through their veins

I hear those sirens in the nighttime

Shadows manipulating the dark

A broken heart from choices made when left alone in the dark

Reflection & Application:

What fears surface for you in the quiet moments of night?

Where has trauma, injustice, or grief shaped how you move through the world?

Daily Affirmation:

I honor my pain without allowing it to define my future.

Meditation Thought:

Awareness brings healing to even the darkest memories.

_____

_____

_____

_____

_____

DAY 17 — ROOTS

Poem:

Down like four flats blood flow of my heart

Mona Lisa Picasso, bond was true art

Thought it was gang forever, roots planted for life

Breath fading looked up surprised that you're the culprit holding the knife

Acceptance of betrayal conflicting with love

Understanding our journey has come to an end, peace elevated from connections to the Sun/Son

Reflection & Application:

Where have you experienced betrayal from those you trusted deeply?

How can acceptance become a pathway to peace rather than resentment?

Daily Affirmation:

I release what has cut me and keep what has shaped me.

Meditation Thought:

Even broken roots can nourish new growth.

_____

_____

_____

_____

_____

DAY 18 — REFLECTION

Poem:

My place of peace as the earth speaks; though the waves may crash, I can calm the seas

I just want to be free

Standing one deep, I am ten toes down

Visions of sunshine, rain, and fire because heavy is the crown

I just want to be free

Reflection & Application:

What does freedom truly mean to you — emotionally, spiritually, or mentally?

Where can you stand firm while still allowing life to flow around you?

Daily Affirmation:

I remain grounded even when life becomes heavy.

Meditation Thought:

Peace is found when I stay rooted in who I am.

_____

_____

_____

_____

_____

DAY 19 — MANIFESTATION

Poem:

From seeking to sought after. That is my desire for you.

Speaking life, love, and healing along your journey, but it must come with hard work.

The soil must be prepared, the seeds must be sown.

May your name be honored and respected in rooms before your physical presence arrives.

The ancestors shine their favor when your spirit calls upon them with blessings overload.

From seeking to sought after. That is my desire for you.

Reflection & Application:

What are you actively preparing yourself for right now?

How are your daily actions aligning with the life you desire to manifest?

Daily Affirmation:

I prepare my soil and trust the growth process.

Meditation Thought:

Intentional effort invites intentional outcomes.

_____

_____

_____

_____

_____

_____

DAY 20 — FREEDOM

Poem:

Build the life you live, and live the life you build

Stay focused

This space I am in, I call that FREEDOM

I love that for me

Reflection & Application:

What does freedom look like in your current season of life?

How can you stay focused on building what truly matters to you?

Daily Affirmation:

I am actively creating a life that feels free and aligned.

Meditation Thought:

Freedom grows where intention and action meet.

_____

_____

_____

_____

_____

PHASE THREE

GROWTH & HEALING

DAY 21 — SAND

Poem:

Be the sand

The sand is a connecting balance between the chaos of seas and the destruction of land

Be the sand

The sand is a cosmic force willing to accept the beatings from nature as it blows, yet it remains calm and still

Be the sand

The sand is not rooted to anything nor anyone. It remains adaptable and flows as the breeze of life transports it from coast to coast

Be the sand

The sand is a welcome kiss of enlightenment upon the lips of crashing waves

Be the sand

I apologize in advance to those whom I may encounter in this next phase of life who may be in their sand phase. Why?

Because I just became the waves

Reflection & Application:

Where in your life are you being asked to remain adaptable rather than rigid?

What does it mean for you to accept change without losing your center?

Daily Affirmation:

I remain grounded while allowing life to move me.

Meditation Thought:

Flexibility is a form of strength.

_____

_____

_____

_____

_____

DAY 22 — WAVES

Poem:

YOU MAY NOW CALL ME ... WAVES!

For the waves are a powerful entity.

The wave connects the world.

The wave has depth unknown.

The wave brings life.

The wave inspires.

The wave is a sustaining life force and home to a world of souls.

The waves bring sustenance to those within and provides for those beyond its reach.

The waves are a passionate force.

For when the sea speaks, heed the warning of the waves.

The very waves that provide a place of peace, can also provide a dangerous grave.

Reflection & Application:

Where do you feel your power expanding in this season of life?

How can you honor both your strength and your responsibility?

Daily Affirmation:

I respect my power and use it with wisdom.

Meditation Thought:

Strength and gentleness can exist together.

_____

_____

_____

_____

_____

DAY 23 — PROCESS AND PAIN

Poem:

Sometimes you have to endure the process and pain of life with a million wrongs, just to prepare you for the glory of that one right.

Crazy part is... that one right could be in your life the entire time, but you are not in position to fully accept and appreciate it yet.

The process is designed to make your inner being grow.

Grow in peace, love and joy so that you can truly enjoy life.

The way you were designed to.

Reflection & Application:

What "process" are you currently in, even if it feels uncomfortable?

How might this season be preparing you for something greater?

Daily Affirmation:

I trust the process shaping my growth.

Meditation Thought:

Pain often prepares the heart for joy.

_____

_____

_____

_____

_____

DAY 24 — WAKE UP AMERICA

Poem:

Your perception of reality is based upon your upbringing. For years, you have been programmed to think and feel a certain way about certain races. Due to mass media, history of events, generational stories and experiences on a conscious and non-conscious level.

These numbers will continue to increase, and our communities will continue to be destroyed until we learn what true love for God and our fellow human brothers and sisters is.

Until we realize that it is simply not about us.

Until we stop being so damn greedy and selfish.

Until we stop allowing the media and government to spoon feed us their agenda.

Until we learn to truly serve one another.

Until we learn to accept one another.

Until we abandon the crabs in a bucket mentality.

Until we learn what hard work and dedication is.

Until we learn to stop making excuses for the way we live our lives.

Until we learn what true equality is.

Until we learn that in order to change the system, we have to first change ourselves.

Until we learn to accept each other's views on life and experiences.

Until we learn not to discredit one another based upon our personal feelings and beliefs ...

things will continue to get worse.

There's a war going on ... physically, spiritually, mentally, and emotionally;

inside our races, between our races ... and my people ...

We are losing the fight.

Reflection & Application:

What beliefs or narratives have shaped how you see others or the world?

Where can you choose empathy, service, and self-awareness over division?

Daily Affirmation:

I choose awareness, compassion, and responsibility.

Meditation Thought:

Real change begins within.

_____

_____

_____

_____

_____

DAY 25 — LION'S ROAR

Poem:

Elegant yet Dangerous,

Docile yet Powerful

Risk-taking yet Calculated and Patiently Methodical

Loving Provider and Protector yet Force of Destruction when necessary

Hear Him Speak.

Feel His Presence.

Embrace His Power.

Welcome to the era of ... me.

Reflection & Application:

How do you balance gentleness with strength in your life?

Where are you stepping fully into who you were meant to become?

Daily Affirmation:

I embody strength, wisdom, and purpose.

Meditation Thought:

Power expressed with intention becomes leadership.

_____

_____

_____

_____

_____

_____

DAY 26 — I AM KING

Poem:

A KING shall RISE!

From the shadows I emerge!

My vibe is the foundation upon which my throne is secured!

I AM ... KING!

Reflection & Application:

What parts of yourself are you finally ready to claim without apology?

Where are you stepping out of the shadows and into your full identity?

Daily Affirmation:

I rise fully into who I am meant to be.

Meditation Thought:

Claiming myself is an act of courage.

_____

_____

_____

_____

_____

DAY 27 — CHEERS

Poem:

Here's to celebrating life, love, wisdom, growth, peace, knowledge, maturity and reaping the harvest of the land

Here's to knowing who you are, walking in your worth, protecting your peace, and never diminishing your light for others

Reflection & Application:

What milestones—big or small—deserve celebration in your life right now?

How can you honor your growth without minimizing it?

Daily Affirmation:

I celebrate my journey and honor my progress.

Meditation Thought:

Gratitude amplifies joy.

_____

_____

_____

_____

_____

DAY 28 — LEGACY

Poem:

Art is Life just as Life is Art. Every breath I breathe, step I take, and move I make, is another chaotic and impactful stroke of creativity.

I have painted many amazing pieces of individual artwork over the years. But in true artistic fashion, the vision will not be completely visible to the public as a full collection until my eternal demise.

My legacy will show an amazing collection of individual artwork that when combined, create the most beautiful piece of art this world will ever see ...

This is Life ...

This, this is KING.

Reflection & Application:

What kind of legacy are you creating through your daily actions?

How do your choices today contribute to the story you'll leave behind?

Daily Affirmation:

My life is meaningful, intentional, and impactful.

Meditation Thought:

Legacy is built moment by moment.

_____

_____

_____

_____

_____

DAY 29 — VICTORY

Poem:

If it's worth it, it won't come easy.

Challenges in life come to expand our territory and our greatness.

Push through.

Your victory is on the other side.

Reflection & Application:

What challenge are you currently pushing through?

How might perseverance be shaping your next breakthrough?

Daily Affirmation:

I continue forward, knowing victory awaits.

Meditation Thought:

Endurance reveals strength.

_____

_____

_____

_____

_____

DAY 30 — REFLECTION (PART 2)

Poem:

Some days I must stop, breathe, and reflect on life.

I must reflect on my accomplishments, get mentally locked in and align my vibes with the world that I choose to create.

My growth, empire, and legacy depend on my ability to trust the process.

I must remind myself that at an early age I have already accomplished every major life goal that I set for myself.

I understand that I have set high standards and hard to obtain goals. For I am my own toughest critic and my own worst enemy.

I must remind myself that I have been set apart for a purpose and journey, that only I can complete.

I must remind myself to relax, not to be so hard on myself, and to truly enjoy life.

I must remind myself that I am now working towards those things that I desire but could honestly live without.

I must remind myself not to settle for anything less than what I deserve in any area of my life.

Daily I must adjust my crown and keep climbing higher in life's ultimate purpose.

Reflection & Application:

How can reflection help you recognize both your growth and your humanity?

What reminders do you need to give yourself more often?

Daily Affirmation:

I honor my progress and trust my path.

Meditation Thought:

Reflection realigns me with purpose.

_____

_____

_____

_____

_____

_____

DAY 31 — BLACK MAN

Poem:

BLACK MAN!

You are a God by Nature

You are strong and moral by Nature

You are kind, respectable, and merciful by Nature

You are a product of peace and righteousness.

Do not take on the identity of a beast just to deny your identity as a God.

Your royalty is in your righteousness.

It is time for us to change the narrative and remind the world of the power that we possess.

We must show them that honest, loving, faithful, hardworking, black men are royalty and do still exist.

Our future generations are depending on us to lead them to victory.

Reflection & Application:

What narratives about yourself or your identity are you ready to challenge or rewrite?

How can you lead—by example, integrity, and love—for those who come after you?

Daily Affirmation:

I walk in dignity, righteousness, and purpose.

Meditation Thought:

My identity is rooted in truth, not labels.

_____

_____

_____

_____

_____

DAY 32 — SCARS

Poem:

My scars tell a story of my struggles, my pain, my healing my growth, my survival, my strengths, my peace, my love, my determination and ultimately, God's grace.

They are my journey.

They are my perseverance.

They are my life.

I am thankful for my scars.

For they made me who I am.

Reflection & Application:

Which scars—seen or unseen—have shaped your strength?

How can gratitude transform the way you view your past wounds?

Daily Affirmation:

My scars are symbols of survival and strength.

Meditation Thought:

Healing honors every part of my story.

_____

_____

_____

_____

_____

DAY 33 — SACRIFICE

Poem:

I sacrificed for this

I prayed for this

I slept in my car for this

I went hungry for this

I endured dark paths for this

I worked for this

I lost those close to me for this

I faced struggles and pain for this

I believe in this

I held God at His word for this

This life I live was destined for me and me only

Reflection & Application:

What sacrifices have shaped the life you are building today?

How can you honor the cost without carrying resentment?

Daily Affirmation:

I honor the sacrifices that carried me here.

Meditation Thought:

Purpose often requires surrender before fulfillment.

_____

_____

_____

_____

_____

DAY 34 — THREE YEARS AGO

Poem:

3 years ago today, the journey began

3 years ago today, lives were forever changed

3 years ago today, our smiles shined bright

3 years ago today, life seemed to get better

3 years later, our journey is ending

3 years later, our lives have been forever changed

3 years later, our hearts and smiles shine bright for a different reason

3 years later, we walk separate paths

It's frustrating yet peaceful to know that 16 days from now we will forever live as strangers.

It has been a learning experience that I will never regret nor change.

It has made me a stronger and better man.

It has allowed me to refocus on myself, truly, and live in a place of peace and joy, full of love for God, life, others, and myself.

I thank God for those 3 years, for they made me who I am.

Reflection & Application:

What season of your life has ended but still shaped you deeply?

How can you honor the growth without clinging to the past?

Daily Affirmation:

I honor every season that formed me.

Meditation Thought:

Endings can be both painful and sacred.

_____

_____

_____

_____

_____

_____

DAY 35 — MASTERMIND

Poem:

I am not human.

I am a higher entity of passion and thrill, of mystique and rage, of tranquility and love.

I am cosmic energy, tapping into the master's mind, to mastermind the masses mind, simply because, my own mind has been dominated by the master's mind.

I am not human.

Reflection & Application:

Where do you tap into creativity, intuition, or inspiration beyond logic?

How do you honor the depth and complexity of your inner world?

Daily Affirmation:

My mind and spirit move in powerful alignment.

Meditation Thought:

Creative energy flows when I trust my inner guidance.

_____

_____

_____

_____

_____

DAY 36 — LET IT BURN

Poem:

I will endure the fire for what means the most to me.

There's a fire burning deep inside of me that motivates me to show the world just how much of a fire I am.

I have the power to bring life or destroy the opposition in my path.

For my passions, I am willing to let it all burn.

Reflection & Application:

What passion burns so deeply inside you that it fuels your perseverance?

Where are you being asked to endure discomfort for the sake of purpose?

Daily Affirmation:

I honor my fire and direct it with intention.

Meditation Thought:

Sacred fire refines rather than consumes.

_____

_____

_____

_____

_____

DAY 37 — FLAWED NOT

Poem:

One of the hardest lessons I had to learn and adjustments I had to make, was holding people to their reality instead of the potential I saw inside of them.

I had to apply this to all relationships; family, friends, intimate romances, and business.

I realized that the pain and struggles I would face within those relationships was partially self-inflicted, because I kept falling for the potential Vs the reality.

As I learned the process of healing and fully walking in my peace, I learned that many people intentionally walk in their brokenness, and I had to decide to no longer allow those types of people to influence my life, my energy, my peace, and my joy.

Yes, we are all flawed humans, but we are not all broken.

Dig deeper, there is a difference.

Reflection & Application:

Where have you confused potential with reality in your relationships?

How can discernment help protect your peace moving forward?

Daily Affirmation:

I honor truth over illusion.

Meditation Thought:

Clarity is an act of self-love.

_____

_____

_____

_____

_____

_____

DAY 38 — THE WRONG RIGHT ONE

Poem:

I thought you were the one. My heart was cold. Black rose wilting in the winter

So much pain led to isolation and withdrawal

Your presence brought the sunshine and opened a world of new possibilities

What felt right, felt like forever

You became my peace, and I became your comfort

We began a journey of growth seemingly unmatched and not disturbed by the chaos of life

However, life became an intricate dance of balance and battle

Peace became war. A war within. A war to remain afloat and cling to each other

Nevertheless, we began to drift

Drift apart as the waves of life intensified their crash against our bond

Now as the anger subsides, I must decide

Do I remain the hero or embrace the villain

Do I embrace the hope or revel in the darkness that has overtaken my heart

Where does the journey go from here?

Reflection & Application:

What relationship felt right but ultimately revealed deeper lessons?

How do you choose hope without denying your pain?

Daily Affirmation:

I allow love to teach me without hardening my heart.

Meditation Thought:

Growth often follows emotional crossroads.

_____

_____

_____

_____

_____

_____

DAY 39 — LET IT GO

Poem:

You can never truly advance in your various areas of life if you keep holding on to what you have grown used to.

Stop taking the expectations and beliefs from your past into the next level that God is trying to grow you.

Let It Go!

Free yourself to elevate yourself, because, believe it or not, some opportunities in life do not always come back around.

Embrace The Change!

Enjoy the new thing he is doing in, through, and to your life.

You are not the same person, and you deserve every bit of life that He is growing you through and to.

Let It Go!

Reflection & Application:

What are you holding onto that no longer serves your growth?

What freedom becomes possible when you release it?

Daily Affirmation:

I release the past and step into what's next.

Meditation Thought:

Release creates space for renewal.

_____

_____

_____

_____

_____

DAY 40 — PEACE, LOVE, JOY, AND LIFE

Poem:

In order to fully experience the benefits of them collectively, you must first be secure in and honor the process it takes to achieve them individually.

You cannot have one without the other.

Reflection & Application:

Which of these—peace, love, joy, or life—needs more attention in your journey right now?

How can honoring the process bring balance?

Daily Affirmation:

I cultivate peace, love, joy, and life with patience.

Meditation Thought:

Wholeness is built one step at a time.

DAY 41 — TRUE LOVE

Poem:

True love is finding that one person who will love you for being you but will also challenge you to grow beyond what you thought possible.

That person who is willing to stand and fight with you, fight by you, and fight for you.

That person that sees beyond your past pain and points you toward our father, God, to be healed.

That person who is strong when you are weak.

That person that will be there at your lowest and celebrate with you at your highest.

That person that God created for you.

Ultimately, it is that person that YOU choose to make a lifelong commitment to and strive daily to honor that commitment.

In case you didn't know that love may not always come from a romantic source.

That love may need to come from inside of you.

Reflection & Application:

How do you define true love in your life today?

Where are you being called to love yourself more deeply?

Daily Affirmation:

I am worthy of love that grows me.

Meditation Thought:

Love begins within.

_____

_____

_____

_____

_____

DAY 42 — DEAR AMERICA ...

Poem:

Dear America, we are not all the same.

Learn our history, learn our pain, learn our purpose, learn the reasons for our pride, learn to understand our struggle, and one day, you may understand and even accept our actions, missions, and goals.

Maybe then you will understand what it means to be Black in America.

Walk where we walk, see what we see, feel what we feel, hear what we hear. Our skin defines us.

It is our blessing, our honor, and our untimely demise.

It may not be the only factor deciding our fate in this world, but it sure does hold a heavy weight on the end result.

Know your own history and understand that what you have seen, were taught consciously and subliminally, the stories and mindsets that were passed down to you, the benefits of your skin in this world that were passed to you from generations prior, the government that was established for YOU, not US, is not OUR history.

Therefore, we fight and protest to change a world that has yet to fully understand and accept us as equals.

We have not said that other lives do not matter. We have not said that others are not hurting. The media that you control said those things.

All we're saying is ...

Dear America, we are not all the same.

Reflection & Application:

How can awareness, listening, and empathy reshape the way you engage with others?

What responsibility do you carry in creating a more just and compassionate world?

Daily Affirmation:

I choose awareness, empathy, and truth.

Meditation Thought:

Understanding is a bridge toward healing.

_____

_____

_____

_____

_____

FINAL REFLECTIONS & GRATITUDE

Take a moment to reflect on the journey you've completed.

What patterns have you released?

What truths have surfaced?

What strength did you rediscover within yourself?

Healing is not linear.

Growth is not perfect.

Peace is not permanent—but it is always accessible.

Honor how far you've come.

Carry forward what you've learned.

Continue choosing yourself, your healing, and your purpose.

Thank yourself for showing up.

Thank life for the lessons.

Thank love for remaining.

— Duane E. Davis II

Made in the USA
Coppell, TX
19 January 2026

67916218R00066